Tip the Scale

Make Moves for Permanent Results

Mervis J Miller II

ISBN: 9780578682259

Acknowledgments

I would first like to acknowledge my wife, Thailand. Thank you for being my biggest supporter. In an effort to be efficient, I would like to consolidate my statement by saying this book is dedicated to Every Business Partner and Barber at Chop It Up Barbershop. We continue to move forward, and I can truly say that I'm very grateful for everything that you all individually and collectively bring to the table. I would also like to give special thanks to the past, present, and future clients of Chop It Up Barbershop. Without your continuous support, we would not be where we are. Thank you to all family members and friends that have helped shape my perspective on life. Thank you, HarborView Medical Center, and all the doctors that contributed to my recovery. Appropriately, I would like to thank God for all the blessings.

About the Author

Mervis J Miller II was Born in the state of Georgia. During high school, he moved to Washington. After Graduating From North West Family Academy, he embarked on achieving his lifelong mission of becoming a Barbershop Owner and Founding Chop It Up Barbershop in 2005. After having substantial success in the Barber Industry, he went on to become a Certified Barber Instructor. Since, Mervis has expanded into other ventures, including the Real Estate Industry and Co-Founding Zawadi Spirits.

Preface

Sitting on the wet grass leaning on a chain-linked fence of someone's front yard in the early hours of April 16th, 2006, I'm faced with a conscious decision to live or die. As my breath gets shorter with every inhale, it seems as though I can't even feel the hot lead bullet lodged somewhere in my abdomen. With the combination of the Seattle rain drizzling down and the moonlight shining, this truly feels like a scene out of a movie. I've heard people say that their life flashed in front of their eyes before, but now I can honestly say that because of this moment, I believe anyone who says that.

My entire life flashed at the speed of light in my mind of all the moments from the beginning up until this point. All I could think was, this can't be it. My movie can't be over right now. I have more to do here. I don't want to die yet. With that very thought, my right arm reached up and grabbed the metal yard fence I was propped on. I pulled myself up with all the energy I had to get on my feet. I remember thinking to myself, just 5 minutes ago, I literally jumped this fence with no struggle. And now I can barely stand up. My blood was leaking out dramatically from a graze and one direct gunshot wound to the mid-left side of my back. Because of the angle in which I was positioned upon impact, the bullet broke two ribs hitting my stomach, esophagus, spleen, and other critical organs. This is when I truly realized how oxygen is directly involved with the blood that circulates through our veins. Just a few hours before this, I was out celebrating my first successful year of being in business, and now I'm literally trying to figure out how to get out of this situation. It dawned on me that I should check my pockets for my cell phone, and of course, it's not there.

With a completely empty surrounding and not a soul in sight, it's clear to me that the only option I have is to get over this fence and out of this person's yard, back to the main street. At least on the street, there were streetlights. Lunging the top half of my body over the fence, I'm now straddled with waste down on one side and waste up hanging on the other side of the fence. Gripping the wires that weave together in the structure of the fence, I pull the rest of my body over to fall on the opposite side of the fence out of breath. Thinking how nice it feels to relax as I try to catch my breath, my eyes begin to get weak, and I want to go to sleep. But again, the thought of my family and the people that know me, reading about a man found dead in the morning news quickly gave me another boost of adrenaline and energy. Just in front of me, I can see the street is wet with the reflection of the lights. I decided to reach up once again, grabbing the fence and pulling upward. Once on my feet, I can visually see a car driving slowly on the next block. The thought of this being the opposition that just tried to kill me, I decided to stagger my way up the street to get a better look at the car.

The closer I get to the street, I realize it's a police vehicle. In an effort to not let the car pass by, I speed up to make it just in time before the car passes the corner stop sign. As I jump in front of the car, the blue lights popped on, and the cop gets out with his gun drawn, asking me if I had any weapons. In the middle of my response, I collapse on the ground. Barely able to keep my eyes open and seeing the bright flashing lights, I'm at a place of peace with however this situation turns out. I can hear the cop now asking me my name and speaking to me, but I'm consciously not too concerned about answering his questions and only mumbling, I've been shot as I go in and out of awareness. Before I knew it, a slap to the face mixed with some woman screaming at me asking me my name, I realized it was a paramedic along with it seemed about a thousand other people standing over me. I responded, *"Mervis,"* then she says, *"Ok, Mervis, we are going to get you to the hospital."* At this moment, I had no idea I would be spending the next week in the ICU unit. Prior to this, an ICU moment was just a scene in a TV show or movie scene. Now in the back of the ambulance, I see they are slicing my clothes off, and blood is everywhere.

That's when I said to myself, just let the doctors do what they do, chill. Within an instant, my mind and spirit begin a world tour traveling around and going to all the places I've ever wanted to, one memory of my travel stands out. While gliding just over the surface of the ocean at high speed towards the bright sun, when I look to my left and to my right, there are dolphins jumping in and out of the water alongside me on this journey. That is vividly the memory of what I had seen. They were like soldiers going to war with me, and I was leading them. Once I got to the island somewhere tucked off in a small shack building, I could see my son peacefully asleep, as, during this time, he was thousands of miles across the ocean away from where the incident just happened. With the assurance that he was ok, I continued on my journey and visited a host of other family members as well. During this time travel, my physical body was being operated on. I later discovered I was in a coma. After a few days, I opened my eyes to notice my arms hanging up in slings. The sound of what it seems, a fish tank pumping water, is loud and noisy. They were oxygen tanks on each side of the hospital bed with three tubes from them going into my ribs, I realized they were supplying my oxygen, and I couldn't breathe without them. I made it. I was Steelivin. I got a second chance at life on earth. I glanced over and seen that I had a visitor, and they were sitting asleep. It was my Pops. I closed my eyes, and all I could say to myself was, I can't wait to get back out there. This time, I have a lot more work to do.

Contents

Page Left Blank Intentionally

Chapter 1
Set the Weight

What is a balanced life for you? For some people, it may be about balancing work and personal life while equally engaging in both. For others, it may be about balancing between the things they have done and things that are still pending on their to-do-list, including building spiritual enlightenment with the universe. When I think of a balanced life, I imagine an antique weighing scale with our many dreams and goals filling the hanging buckets on one side and all the obstacles and hurdles on the other.

Throughout our days, we take on weight, saying yes to tasks and deciding to put items into our buckets, often weighing one side down, tipping one side lower than the other. However, if you want to live a balanced life, you must know how to offset the weight on your scale to get what you want accomplished. We spend our lives trying to achieve our goals to lighten the heavier side of the scale, but living a balanced life is not easy. On the other hand, if you think clearly, it is not that difficult to achieve. The reason why there is an entire chapter called set the weight is that without the weight *"meaning agenda,"* you cannot tip the scale. Tipping the scale requires a lot of weight, goals, and ideas. You must know how to tip them in your favor. It involves a plan and execution. The concept of tipping the scale can be extreme in one way or another – positively or negatively. Either way, you will get a result, which dives into the subtitle of the book, make moves for permanent results. Every step that you make towards your goal is important, and planning it all out is vital.

The particular scale that I am referring to is a Balance Scale, and the weight is all your objectives. In life, we come across a lot of people who live their lives with a pretty well-balanced lifestyle. We observe them and their actions but never really realize what they are doing for such balance.

And wonder to ourselves, how can we also create balance in our lives? We can most definitely bring balance to our lives, but if it's too balanced, we can quickly get complacent. The side where all your ambitions rest must always be the heavier one, hurdles should never be the reason for you to stop working towards your holy grail. That is why it is essential to set goals first, and if you do not already know what they are, it is definitely time you start setting them.

Have you ever thought about why it is so important to set goals? Let me explain with an example. Imagine yourself in a situation. It's a nice sunny day. You decide you want to go out but do not know where. You just grab the keys of your car, get out of your home, and start driving aimlessly.

After driving for a while, you feel the sun has gone down, and darkness is taking over, and in no time, it starts to pour down rain. The thunder is striking, the sky is cracking back and forth, and all of a sudden, you find out your car's tire has run flat. You look around and find out that there is not a soul around in sight, not a single shop around, or a car passing by. You do not even know where you exactly are, and on top of it, you left your phone at home.

That is when it hits you that you should have decided a place to go to instead of driving for hours and ending up in the middle of nowhere, or you should have never left your home. Now apply this to your real life. That is precisely the situation we encounter when we do not know in what direction we are supposed to go and just keep going aimlessly. That is the reason why you need to have a road-map, you must know what path to choose, and to be prepared for everything that comes your way, you must know your final goal. Cliché's aside, understanding the importance of setting your goal and knowing how crucial it is to accomplish them is a major key. In case you are still not convinced enough, here are the few reasons why I think it's so important to set goals:

They Propel You Forward

When you know exactly where to go, you are more likely to reach there faster, sort of pushing you forward. You are more likely to make efforts in the right direction. Your goals are an external representation of your inner decisions and thoughts, a constant reminder of what you need to accomplish. It's only when you have a particular goal you would be able to put your mind onto it and be more likely to achieve it.

Boosting Self-Belief

Setting goals for yourself can help fuel your ambition. It is not just about creating a plan for your life and holding yourself accountable. Your goals should always be motivational enough to make you do what you thought was impossible in the first place. It will not only make you want to achieve but also make you believe that you can do it, and eventually, you will.

Turning The Unachievable Into Achievable

A lot of people let go of their biggest dreams, thinking they are impossible to be turned into a reality. It is easy to get discouraged when your dreams are as big as mount rainier, but have you ever tried to make those dreams your only aim? It takes strong will and consistency to do so, and once it is your only goal, it will be easier for you to achieve. That same mount rainier will turn into a walkable hill.

Proper and serious goal setting can turn the entire game around for you and also put the right weight on the balance scale. You can take the mountains you need to climb and break them up into smaller hills that you can walk. You will be happier and more motivated to start working towards that next milestone on your way to greatness.

Helping You Continually Improve

What's the point in improving a little bit each day if you are not growing in the areas that you want to grow in after all? The goals that you define for yourself will inevitably shape you into the person who you want to become. They will develop your character, and they can also help you measure your progress.

Essentially, having small stepping stones to the final destination helps you determine where you started, where you are now, and how much further you need to go. In this manner, your goal setting can serve as milestones and benchmarks that help you determine how well you are progressing towards your most important goals. It keeps you on track and in-check for your own-self, and then you continue to improve.

Setting goals is a road-map to success

The role that setting goals plays in our way to success should be evident by now. It is critical to get you where you want to be. An action plan that shows you where you are going, how you can get there, and what to focus on in your road-map to success is vital to have. Once you have it ready, nothing can hold you back from achieving what you want to accomplish. When you have the plan in your hands, you know exactly where to start and what tools to bring with you. Then all you need to do is engage yourself completely and utilize every opportunity that makes you closer to your end goal. Now that you are well aware of the importance of setting goals, you must know how to set them and where to start. I will not just throw random statements out there without clarity; this book of tools will help you reach where you want to be, at least inside your mind. There has to be a pattern to follow. I am sure by the end of this chapter, you would be able to set goals for yourself and be motivated enough to thoroughly achieve them.

So, how do you set the objectives for yourself? Goal setting is a robust process for thinking about your ideal future, and for motivating yourself to turn your vision of the future into reality. The process of setting goals ultimately takes a certain amount of courage. By knowing what you want to achieve, you will automatically deal with the reality of achieving them or not. This will also help you quickly detect the distractions that can easily lead you astray, and kick them out of your way. Here are the few things that you must consider while setting the Holy Grail for yourself:

Start by Setting Personal Goals

You do not just wake up one morning and decide this is what I want to do in life. You set your goals on several levels. First, you create a big picture of what you want to do with your life or maybe where you want to be in the next ten years. Only then can you identify the large-scale goals that you want to achieve. Second, you break these down into the smaller targets that you must hit to reach your lifetime objectives. You set daily, weekly, monthly, and yearly targets that get you closer to your final destination. Finally, when you have your strategy, you can start working on it without delay.

That is why we start the process of setting goals by looking at your end goals. Then, we work down to the things that we can do in, say, the next five years, next month, next week, tomorrow or today, so begin now.

Set Goals That Motivate You

When you set objectives for yourself, it is crucial that they motivate you enough: this means making sure that they are important to you, and that there is value in achieving them. If you have little interest in the outcome, or they are irrelevant given the bigger picture, then the chances of you putting in the efforts to make it happen are low. Motivation is the key to achieving success in every way of life.

Set SMART Goals

You have probably heard of SMART goals already, but do you always apply the rule? The simple fact is that for targets to be compelling, they have to be SMART. There are many variations of what SMART stands for, but the point is that your goals should be Specific, Measurable, Attainable, Relevant, and Time-Bound.

Setting Specific Goals

Your objectives must be clear and well defined. Vague or generalized ideas of a destination are of no use because they do not provide a clear direction. Remember, you need goals to show you the way not to make it blurry. Make it as easy as you can to get where you want to go by precisely defining where you want to end up.

Set Measurable Goals

Include precise amounts, dates, and so on in your goals so you can measure your degree of success. If your short term goal is simply defined as, 'To reduce expenses,' how will you know when you have achieved success? You will have to measure how much you spent last week or last month to how much you are spending now. Without a way to measure your success, you miss out on the celebration that comes with knowing you have achieved something.

Set Attainable Goals

Make sure that the ambitions you have set are possible for you to achieve. If you set an objective that you have no hope of achieving, you will only demoralize yourself and erode your confidence.

However, resist the urge to set objectives that are too easy. Accomplishing a goal that you did not have to work hard for will be of no value in your eyes, and the day you achieve it may seem to you like any other ordinary day. It can also make you fear setting future targets that carry a risk of failure. By setting realistic, yet challenging goals, you hit the balance you need. These are the types of goals that require you to raise the bar, and they bring the greatest personal satisfaction when achieved.

Set Relevant Goals

Your aim should be relevant to the direction you want your life and career to take. By keeping aims aligned with your personal life, you can easily develop the focus you need to get ahead and do what you want. Set widely scattered and inconsistent targets, and you will squander your time and your life away.

Set Time-Bound Goals

Your landing place must have a deadline. Again, this means that you know when you can celebrate success. When you are working on a deadline, your sense of urgency increases, and achievement comes to you much quicker.

Set Goals in Writing

Having a written target gives you a sense of satisfaction and something to plan and work for. The physical act of writing down an objective makes it real and tangible. You have no excuse for forgetting about it. The choice of words here matters a lot. As you write, use the word 'will' instead of 'would like to' or 'might.' For example, *"I will reduce my operating expenses by 10% this year,"* not *"I would like to reduce my operating expenses by 10% this year."* The first statement has power, and you can picture yourself reducing expenses, the second lacks passion and gives you an excuse if you get off the track.

Post your goals in visible places to remind yourself every day of what it is that you intend to achieve. Put them on your walls, desk, computer monitor, bathroom mirror, or refrigerator as a constant reminder. I use my alarm clock on my phone for that; it works great for me because it interrupts me and reminds me when I'm not even thinking about my goals.

Make an Action Plan

This step often is ignored in the process of goal-setting. You get so focused on the outcome that you even forget planning all the steps needed along the way. By writing out the individual steps, and then crossing each one off as you complete it, you will realize that you are making progress towards the end of the line. It is especially crucial if your eventual goal is big and demanding or long-term.

Stick With It

Remember that goal setting is an ongoing activity, and it is not meant to end. Set built-in reminders to keep yourself on track, and make regular time-slots available to review your progress. Your end destination may remain quite similar over the long term, but the action plan you set for yourself along the way can change significantly. Make sure the relevance, value, and necessity remain high.

Therefore, it is essential to set goals and knowing how to set them in order to live a life that makes a difference. It's time that you must gather all the equipment and start working towards your ultimate goal. Think clearly and then decide where you want to head. Do not let the fear of failure take over your ambitions. Listen to your inner voice and START TAKING YOURSELF SERIOUSLY. When was the last time you took yourself seriously? When was the last time you got excited about an idea you had but then never pursued it because you decided it was not good enough? When was the last time you started to make something but gave up mid-way before you even finished because you did not think anyone would like it?

If you could remember yourself in a certain situation while reading all these questions, it means you have been there, of course. Whenever you do not make time to celebrate your little achievements and honor what is meaningful to you, you are not taking yourself seriously. Whenever you dispel positive feedback, mentally or in reality, you are not taking yourself seriously.

Whenever you tell yourself that your dreams are nice and all, but they are unrealistic, you are not taking yourself seriously. Whenever you do not make time for self-care, talk yourself out of a great opportunity, fail to share all the real things you are doing, and creating in your life, and whenever you talk yourself down, you are not taking yourself seriously.

What happens when you do not take yourself seriously is that you sabotage yourself. You rush through a half-hearted execution and do not give yourself the time you need to learn something new or do it the right way. When things do not go the way you wanted them to, you start believing that it was never worth it. You get depressed. You get angry and disappointed with yourself. You wonder why you have not done anything yet. To avoid all of that, you must take yourself seriously. You are reading this now because I took the idea of writing this book seriously.

Here's why the world needs you to start taking yourself seriously: Every book you read, every piece of music you listen to, every movie you watch, every app you use, every website you visit, every gadget you use, every building you visit, everything man-made that you experience, every major sports event you've attended or watched on TV, they exist because, at some point, at least one person took themselves seriously. They had too even when others around them did not. We all have ideas in our heads that we never tell anyone thinking nobody would care, or they are not good enough. If you always had something at the back of your mind, it's time that you bring it to the front.

Any and everyone who lives this life and would like to participate in the daily hustle and bustle, to achieve and acquire capital, property, or possession, will have to take themselves seriously first. If you do not take yourself seriously, you will never be able to pursue your dreams.

When deciding and setting your goals, you must listen to what your heart and mind are telling you out of the gate. It may sound cliché, but if you do not take yourself seriously, no one else will. It surprises me how many people get mad at others when they tell people what their plans are, and People just shrug them off. They say, *"Okay!"* or *"Oh, Okay, let me know when you do that,"* and they may chuckle. When, in fact, you should not expect all of them to believe a word you say until they know you. They do not need to know you personally; they just need to know your reputation.

Now, what is your reputation? Are you known as someone who gets things done? Or are you known as a procrastinator? It is time to set your reputation right. When you set your goals, it will be imperative to make sure it is your life's mission to achieve it. Remember, if you do not achieve the goals you set, it will be hard for you or anyone else to believe in you. Most things you have ever imagined are lit with possibilities. Give yourself some time to figure it out. It can be something like speaking up at work, or it might mean just finishing that one thing you have been thinking about forever. Or it might mean tweeting about it, making a video or blog post about it, or getting on a stage and sharing it with an audience. Ultimately, When you are focused enough, others can then take you seriously. You will put your ideas out there instead of hiding them. You would not delete them. You will keep trying because you and your ideas are important and have the potential to become so much more than you realize. When ideas start to materialize, people can identify with them more easily.

Being believable takes time to establish in the community. Trust is earned just like a paycheck. People will believe you whenever you work for their trust. Trust plays a vital role in being believable. When people believe in you, they become a part of your success as well. They can be proud to tell others how they were a part of your journey to success. With trust and belief in you and your brand, you also gain access to your supporters' resources, be it capital, relationships, or information, etc. Either way, your supporters will ultimately hold you accountable and responsible for achieving *"Your"* goals. At the back of your mind, you must always know they are watching, and they are waiting. Your honor, your word, and your taking yourself seriously are all key factors in achieving the goals you set. Again, a sense of accomplishment is important; therefore, make sure that your objectives are reasonable and realistic. So when you start to set your aim, you must keep that in mind at all times that this is what I want to do.

Who doesn't want to be honored? To be trusted? To be successful? We all want to, but it takes time and effort. So, to achieve your goals, you must take care of certain things:

Intend to Commit\

No matter what your life goal is or where you want to be, if there is no commitment, there is no success. You need to plan every step, and you should be genuinely willing to make things happen.

Make a Plan

I have said this more than once, and I will keep repeating it; Planning is important in every aspect of life. Therefore, MAKE A PLAN!

Tell the World

The minute you decide that you are ready to commit to a goal, be it changing careers, getting in shape, or finding more time for travel or family, tell everyone what you intend to do. The more people you tell, the more you are obligated to follow through with your goals.

Get Organized

Once you have made the intention to commit, told the world about your plans, and have a plan in hand, get yourself organized. What tools do you need to make things happen? It's time to eliminate all the noise in your life and focus on what's important. Utilize your time and money in the direction of your goal.

Define your fears

Think about what you are putting off for the 'right moment.' What holds you back? What are you afraid of? Write down the worst things that might happen if you fail, then think about what you will do if they happen and how you could prevent them. This can help you get over your fears and start taking action.

Create a Support System

It does not matter who you choose for your support system, but make sure you have people to rely on. Family and friends can be great motivators, but sometimes you need to look outside that circle and get professional help. You just need to know when you should ask for their help. You cannot waste time thinking who you must approach, therefore, create a support system for yourself.

Speak with Honor

You will notice that to believe in yourself, you have to honor yourself when you speak. Make sure that you believe in what you say to people. Being honorable is being honest, making sure that when you say something to someone, you mean it. You cannot just blubber out things that you are going to do, but never really accomplish. Sometimes telling things to people is good, but even not telling will not hurt you, I believe.

If you do not tell people what you are going to do, then no one gets the opportunity to hold you accountable but yourself. You have to tell people constantly about what you are going to do to exercise your ideas. However, if you do not do it, it does not hurt you. Honor is an extraordinary power that all humans possess. Moving with honor, the world responds to it very well. People begin to believe you and believe 'in' you. This way, as you move forward in achieving the goals you have set, your surroundings will begin to assist you. I hope by now, you understand the concept of setting your weight. I look at the scale as a metaphoric tool in the case of describing how I weigh out life's obstacles and challenges. So yes, when I say *"set the weight,"* I do mean set the goals, meaning put your goals on the scale, to offset what's already on one side, which is life's challenges that we are all born with. We all have our own challenges, but you can tip the scale in your favor by offsetting the circumstances with achieving your goals.

Chapter 2
Get a Scale

How many times have you introduced yourself as: *"Hey, I am a barber, or a doctor, or an engineer?"*

We have become so involved and immersed in our daily work life that when we are posed with the question of who we are, we often respond in work-related terms. Why is that we seem to put our job roles at the forefront instead of prioritizing our sense of self or self-image? I am sure this example is impactful enough to make you realize the gravity of the situation.

Our existence would practically come to a halt if we were to think outside of our professional roles and see life in isolation. Our life is a vast mixture of various experiences, actions, and inaction, paired with work and rest. Work is that one single factor that fills our inner being with creative satisfaction and always gives us something to look forward to. It prevents life from getting too mundane and boring and basically gives us a direction to channel our energies. Had it not been for the work that we do every day, our energies would stay bottled up. They would make us feel all kinds of frustrating vibes, and unused energies often put us in a state of unrest and idleness. Time does not seem to pass and hangs heavy on our shoulders when we are idle. On the other hand, we do not even get to know where our time flies when we are preoccupied with work.

I've always heard, an idle mind is a devil's workshop. When your mind is not preoccupied with anything productive, you tend to direct your energies in places where they are least needed. This can hurt your self-belief or self-sabotage your interests. Sometimes people take up menial jobs or even the kind of work that is not very fulfilling as it is better than not doing anything at all.

The human mind and soul are in a constant quest to achieve new skills and talents and look for ways to be the best version of themselves. Ever since I've been able to pay attention to the way society evolves, I've noticed the one common thing amongst people - the concept of work. Working is the one common language that most people share. Ever since the beginning of time, we as humans have had to work to survive. The motivation to work has to be clear. If your survival depends on your work ethic, you will always be willing to put your all into it.

What Is A Strong Work Ethic?

Work ethic is something that helps you establish yourself and your career on firm grounds. It equips you with the set of values needed to discipline yourself and work hard towards your goal. When you build a strong work ethic, you train yourself to work hard until it becomes a part of second nature, and you just follow through effortlessly.

When you hold work ethics in high reverence, you focus on your work, find ways to stay motivated, and knock out tasks on their respective deadlines – this, in turn, helps establish your credibility. Building credibility will play a major role in your success in the long run. So working hard and being reliable is non-negotiable when it comes to credibility. Your work ethic will become a form of currency for you. Long hours of working hard and helping others with getting things done will ultimately transition into verbal words of currency. Your verbal words will soon be all you need for others to trust as you have already put in so much effort for others to place their trust in you.

The integrity of your work ethics will be dependent on your work attitude towards the day. Having a positive mindset in an environment that you dislike is difficult. So you have to focus on your value as an individual at all times. What value do you bring to the table? Do your peers clearly see your value, or would they not even feel your absence if you were to quit your job? You might hate your job, but it might be possible that your job hates you just as much or even more. This works against you and stays with you in the long term until it chips away at your self-confidence.

You need people from your workplace to hang out with you and have good things to say about you. If it is important to you, it will happen. However, I do not, in any way, intend to say that you need to conform who you are to other people's standards. I'm simply saying that you need to surround yourself with people who'd rather stay silent if they do not have anything positive to say. In continuation of that theory, if you view work as an important and indispensable part of your life, it gets easy to get through the day-to-day grind mentally. Your work environment will play a huge role in acquiring and achieving success.

Without a scale, it's practically impossible to weigh anything effectively. Again, I refer to the scale as a metaphoric tool in this case. It's a must for you to get the tools you'll need to get the work done and accomplish your goals. Your scale are things like a workplace, informational materials such as books, manuscripts, and audiobooks, the equipment you may need to work with, like painting materials, computers, basketball, and last but not least, even your place of peace and relaxation will help.

The place you go to every day after work is important and can be helpful for you to prepare for the following day. Work is the bottom-line basics of everything you achieve. Work can build you up for all kinds of adversity that you come across. The actual physical labor, as well as the intellectual, mental work that you put your brain through. It will consume you to the maximum. It depends on how big your dreams are, on how you go about tipping the scale to weigh out these ideas.

Effect of Environment on Your Productivity

Why is the phrase *"get a Scale"* so important? You need to have a day-to-day regimen – that is where you bring all your problems, ideas, and energies to, every single day. This place cannot be at home, in bed, or on the couch. Unless, of course, your job is equipped for that. This scale should be in an environment that is conducive to learning and growth, that is at a place of work. A work environment – more like a gym for your goals and dreams.

The day you start working on your environment, it brings value to your life by helping you achieve your daily goals. It also helps establish a witness of your endeavors and helps you track your progress by working around others.

A part of it is for others to watch your struggles – the plight of showing up to work when you do not want to. This is when people can start believing in your dreams and vice versa. Your work environment might not be the ideal place to be, but this is what you have to do to get things done. You need to find a way to make this place bearable and fun until you are able to move your energies to somewhere more beneficial to your goals. If your space at home is chaotic, you should find your comfort zone at a coffee café or someplace near outdoor Nature, where you can cut off all the clutter and the noise and concentrate after a long day for a few hours. The point of this is to relax and think after you spend the majority of your day in the game, on the court, on the field, and have engulfed yourself in what you're attempting to accomplish.

During your grind, you basically have to be obsessed with achieving your goals, so the environments you spend most of your time in must help bring this to pass. Imagine trying to record a song without recording equipment, or trying to build a house without a piece of property to start the construction. Everything is that simple; try not to over-complicate this. If you do not have the means to gather all of the materials, you will need to get things done, then that simply means you will need to work and build up your toolbox.

How You Acquire Things Will Determine Your Inner Energy

The idea of asking others to provide the means or donate to your cause can be a mistake in this process, unfortunately. These times we are living in are very competitive, in my opinion. Everyone that you would involve outside of your inner circle is most likely working on their own problems and projects, so you will only create discomfort when they have to associate with you by asking for a handout. You must accept the fact that if you do not have, then you will have to work to get. The only exception to this is if you are entitled to an inheritance or family members are obligated by way of

DNA to help you establish your career. You will regret taking short cuts. Most likely, You will also hear it from whomever you've accepted help from that you would not be there without their support.

This could drastically undermine your mental health and manifest itself in the form of low-self-esteem and a lack of self-belief. A self-made person will always internalize positive feelings about themself. They will be able to present their confidence because they know that wherever they are today is only because of their efforts. Being dependent on someone in your initial years will only put you through the ordeal of owing your success to someone when, in reality, it was you who made all the sacrifices. It's not a very uplifting feeling to getting to hear that your success is not entirely yours to own.. In America, some organizations were designed to assist the less fortunate as well. That could very well be an option for you, as long as your pride will allow it. Many people in the world will help you and not think twice about bringing it up and taking credit for it. On the other hand, some people would never speak of what they've done to help you. But it's rare to find those kinds of people in today's world as everyone wants to take credit for their contribution to people's lives.

If I consider myself, for instance, I usually seek other's help as the last resort so that I do not be a burden on them. This also keeps my expectations low, and my friends and family do not get burdened unnecessarily. It is not wrong or bad to seek help, but if you can manage your resources on your own accord and become self-sufficient, there is nothing like it. It also enhances your reputation and image amongst colleagues and friends. It goes unsaid that independence certainly does create a positive image of yourself in your eyes as well as the other person.

I've found it to be helpful for me, mainly to avoid later accusations, as if I needed help. Taking help from someone always gives them an upper hand, and they can sometimes choose to treat you the way they want. I'm a firm believer in making something out of nothing. The world is a vast field full of untapped opportunities that we can venture into. It's just that we never take the time or look deep enough. We do think of great ideas, but the limitations in our minds bound us to take the simplest way of doing things to follow it through. In this modern era of the internet, increasing our level of self-awareness is very important to excel in life. I do believe this is possible because I've done it.

However, I've also regretted accepting help from friends and even family members that were not in sync with my overall vision. Sometimes, we have this illusion that if we take the support of people around us, it will be easier to rise up the ladder. However, it can be equivalent to self-sabotaging your own goals as you plunge into the deep conflict-ions of the world. I've heard the term, just take the stairs and forget about the elevator, you'll feel better when you get to the top. One way of accepting help and retaining your integrity is to make it a two-way road. If you are taking help in any form, make sure that you return it with some kind of gesture or a token of appreciation. You can even do something in return as a form of payment.

You can either pay in monetary terms, and if that is not possible or appropriate, you can decide on specific terms that will benefit both parties. Pre-decide the terms and sign a deal. I'll give you an example. When I opened up my first barbershop, I went through a rough time.

My top priority was to keep my doors open for business, and I did not spare any cash for personal purchases. My cash flow income mainly went right back into my business. I was without a vehicle for a while, and I needed some wheels. I spoke about this with a few of my customers, and one of them had an extra car for sale. As I said, I did not have money for a vehicle, so we established a deal.

The pre-decided terms that we agreed on were that I would help the car owner with some janitorial work at the YMCA after work hours at the barbershop. I would do this until my work pay had cleared the price he was charging for the car. I literally worked after work every day for about three months. The deal was done, and I had the means to commute without hassle. As the amount of the loan got offset by the services I was offering, I was relieved of a great burden off my shoulders. He got his work done, and I got the car I needed. This method, I feel, can be used to help you sail through such a situation smoothly. Truth be told, I did not want to do the janitorial work, but it was my scale at the time to get the vehicle. Sometimes, to tip the scale in your favor, you need to make certain changes in your life that will set you on the success trajectory.

The mental portion of acquiring your scale is important because sometimes it can be the most challenging part of your day. We often get so engrossed in our daily goals and targets that we tend to hinder our own growth and progress. Mental stimulation is critical when we are overburdened with a lot of commitments, and we have no option but to ask for a helping hand. It is how steadfast we stay in the face of these challenges and retain our calm in crazy times that decides the final outcome.

Having the Right Mindset

"Everybody wants to be famous, but nobody wants to do the work. I live by that. You grind hard so you can play hard. At the end of the day, you put all the work in, and eventually, it'll pay off. It could be in a year; it could be in 30 years. Eventually, your hard work will pay off."

-Kevin Hart

The mind and thoughts can sometimes make you feel that the entire world is against you. It can be very deceiving. The most important thing to remind yourself of is, what's the motive? What's the reason the world is trying to hold you back. If you think about an issue, attempt to source it. Where does it stem from? Was it something you said or was it something you did? Sometimes that energy can stick to you like a badge of honor.

Everywhere you go, people will see the energy on your face. For example, do your peers see your value, or would your peers be more interested in not being around you at all? You encounter all sorts of personalities in your professional life, some who would be a great assistance in helping you work out your way and tackle any challenges that come your way and even go out of the way to help you settle in and figure things out.

Then there are secret connivers who are always on the lookout to find a reason to pull you down. As we proceed through the day, there is a unique energy that we carry and ultimately share that vibe with the world as well. Energy is something that we embody within us and is ultimately what defines us and how we engage with the world around us. Positive energies help us stay upbeat and vibrant and make any negative feelings of anxiety and frustration fizzle out into thin air. If the energy around you is toxic and negative, it breeds discomfort, mistrust, and resentment. Hence, your ultimate goal should attract positive energy and block any negative energy that seems to surround you. Every influence and energy in your surroundings will ultimately shape your mindset and help you through life's difficulty with ease.

Again, I am, by no means, telling you to change your character to accommodate others. I'm merely saying that you should either surround yourself with people who prefer to stay silent if they have nothing positive to say or are looking to work as a team to figure out differences. This is because the influence around you does have a profound impact on how you view life and, ultimately, your overall credibility and reputation.

Furthermore, it will play a significant role in your future achievements. When people see you have a positive aura around you and all the hard work that you have put in to build your credibility, it makes it easier for them to place their trust in you. Your scale determines your vision. So It has to be very clear, and the target has to be on point so that you are fully prepared to take control of your life. It's important to stay loyal to the path you have chosen and know that there is no going back once you have embarked on a specific journey.

Say, for example, if you want to become the best football player in town, you need to have the right environment to train, a professional trainer, and a deep-seated interest and motivation to propel you to reach unprecedented heights. Once you establish the right environment that is productive to learning, and you are in it every day, it's easy to focus. It all comes together when you make a routine and get all the elements discussed above in synch and – getting the mindset together, setting your schedule, being determined to do whatever you have to do.

All these concepts play their respective parts in cementing the idea of tipping the scale in your favor. You need to have that presence of mind and the ability to prioritize things that will help you weigh out the things that do not matter and pull you down unnecessarily. The main objective is to Have that peace of mind when you go home at night.

When attempting to be a responsible person and someone who prioritizes hard work and instills the right values in your life while religiously following them, you will know that there is no short cut to success. To reach a certain point in your life, you need to be mentally and physically prepared to take up every challenge that comes your way.

Many people expect to get things done without working for it, and that's just not negotiable when your aims are lofty. Often people shun away from hard work because the truth is that hard work is 'hard.' Many reasons make us run away from hard work in the way, and it's highly likely that we are not specifically motivated or engrossed enough to put our all in the current job role that we are serving.

None of us like to work too much on something that does not interest us. You want to have something you are passionate about. It is essential to have high regard for yourself and know why you are doing something by keeping it at the forefront at all times. Your work environment has to display why you're doing something. Whether you hit the target or slightly miss, you have to reassess and reevaluate your vision and keep updating your goals in your mind. Work may not necessarily be fun or motivating all the time, but we have to find creative ways to keep the connection alive and not give up due to tough times or stagnancy. The alternative to hard work is simply not palatable if you want to reach your desired destination.

Conclusively when I say Get a Scale it focuses merely on:

- Work ethics
- Getting the right environment
- Getting the right mindset
- Gathering the tools you need

Chapter 3
Weigh it Up

"Identity is a prison you can never escape, but the way to redeem your past is not to run from it, but to try to understand it, and use it as a foundation to grow."

–Jay Z

It's human nature to find faults in ourselves and to feel the weight of it pulling us down. There are many things that we intend to accomplish in so many areas of our life, which we think need improvement. However, upon retrospection, I have realized that although I may not be the best version of myself that I had envisioned to be and still have a long way to go, I, as a human, need to acknowledge the progress! The progress, even if it's just a short distance, is what matters and should be recognized.

We do not have the habit of giving ourselves the due credit for achieving whatever we have in life and celebrating the little victories in life that make us who we are. We should be proud of ourselves for breaking free from habits that undermine our truc potential, having the mental capacity to let go of toxic relationships, and having the audacity to step out of comfort zones. If we begin to feel the magnitude of these little moments, life would be much smoother and more relaxed. Everyone has a life story of their own and is fighting their own battles, and to realize that you have given your all to reach the status where you are today, you need to internalize the feeling that success doesn't just happen to you overnight. You need to go through the series of struggles, hardships, and setbacks that make you who you are. Before you invest your mental and physical energies in someone else, you need to forge that bond with yourself – and feel the difference.

It's not only about developing your mental capacity but also realizing how much you have grown as a person. If we evaluate ourselves on a scale of self-perception, the realization of how much we have evolved can be intimidating and enlightening at the same time. It can be scary and limit our ability to think beyond the realms of practicality and visualize our growth beyond normal limits. However, each one of us has an innate ability to catapult our lives in the direction that we've always wanted. We are all doing something or the other in our lives that can help us take inspiration from our journey and growth so far in our lives. Think about it like this. When you are born as an infant, can you believe that just nine months before that, you were physically smaller than an ant? Your physical body was smaller than a grain of salt at one point, and before that, your existence practically began from nothing. Here you are now in concrete physical stature, most likely able to look at an ant-like it's practically just an 'ant.' Now imagine if ants could keep growing like humans in physical stature, would you look at them in the same light. No, right? View yourself that way.

Look how far you've come and appreciate the journey that you have taken. Reflect on how long it's taken you to get to the physical stature you've gotten to. Most humans grow in physical stature for about 15-20 years, I suppose. Imagine if you never stop growing? We would be giants and too big for earth. For some people, they feel that they actually never stop growing. Obviously not physically, but psychologically. This brings us to the fact that growing, evolving, transforming, and becoming who you are can be a never-ending journey where there is no limit. You should be your benchmark and set the standard higher for yourself each day. You need to be appreciative of your strengths and journey both.

Persona Building

One thing in life is definitely guaranteed – the more precisely and sooner you discover yourself and your values, the easier it will be for you to build your own persona. This will help you assign the right value to what truly matters and what doesn't. Apply the 'weigh it up' concept. Where you, build and focus on what makes up your entire existence and identify the key components. The stature that you reach, whether physical, emotional, or mental – is your persona. Your persona only grows as much as you allow it to. Most humans establish a view of themselves and their persona and get to a place of comfort.

This is where they think they are the best version of themselves as they feel empowered to do or say whatever they want. When it comes to investing in your persona and polishing it as per the society's standards, there's a lot that you can do and accomplish. The persona can grow and never stop. That's why you have some personas that take up a lot of space.

With certain people, their persona can fill up a room, while some personas may not even be noticeable in that same room. This is kind of like trying to locate an 'ant' at Time Square on New Year's Eve. Could you imagine that? It would probably be impossible. This example is to make you feel and visualize the impact of certain personalities whose presence and absence can be felt. Everyone has their own unique aura around their personalities.

Every personality emanates a certain level and kind of energy that is formulated based on the experiences that the person has undergone and how it influences their presence. Having a positive personal presence is a conscious choice. Your presence in a room or in a social gathering has different connotations, including your feelings and emotions, and how you leverage them to interact with people and leave an ever-lasting impression.

It is human nature to figure out the vibes the other person is giving out before you indulge in any sort of communication. This requires you to sharpen your sensory awareness as well as your cognitive abilities to ensure that people stay uplifted and feel safe in your presence. To elaborate on the concept of personas and the individual presence that you have in a social setting, let me give you an example. Take the most famous person you know, and then you take, let's say, your kindergarten teacher. Put them both in Disney World. You are given the task of locating them, and when you are on this mission, you will soon realize that it's way easier to spot the person with more popularity than someone who is not very known. Most likely, you would spot the famous person first because of their persona and how it affects all of the other people around them.

People would be all hyped up to have a renowned personality around them and give them their undivided attention, while your kindergarten teacher could be standing right next to you. Because you haven't seen them in so long, you might not even notice them or their persona.

Your persona, in its truest form, is who you are. You can either choose to stay in the same space all your life or always work towards bettering yourself and putting your best foot forward. Alternatively known as 'personal presence' – it is something that is not very straightforward to define, but we can feel it in our surroundings when it is present. A person who has a strong persona will attract energy when they walk into the room, and the overall vibes will revolve around them. When they speak, they speak with so much confidence and conviction that people inevitably pay attention. Most likely, they don't even have to speak, and people can understand them. Positive or Negative. People with a strong presence act according to their surroundings and reflect on their attitudes and emotions before taking the next step.

They have an internal compass of control and believe in projecting their true, genuine selves so that whoever they are, comes from within. There is no facade or mask hiding their true face, trying to be someone they are not. When you do not have to give your behavior a second thought, it means that you have a strong presence as you are a combination of who you are at the core. Their thoughts and actions are in perfect harmony, and there is no discrepancy between them.

This is the significance your persona can have in gaining recognition and a specific position in your life. In order to develop your persona, you need to be cognitively aware, pay attention to other people's opinion of you through their words and body language. This requires you to be both inwardly and outwardly aware so that you are not unnecessarily influenced by other people's judgments and know what you want to project in life.

Investing In Your Persona

Some people invest in their persona for their lives while others stop investing in their persona at certain ages or levels in their journey. Your persona is the one thing that all of us, as humans, have, which can grow beyond the physical stature. So, you have to feed it! Everyone has a persona that defines their 'ideal self.'

In psychological terms, there is a self-discrepancy theory that enlightens us about how we all have a picture of our 'ideal self' painted in our minds, which inevitably motivated us to improve, change and be the best version of ourselves each day. The clearer the picture you have of yourself, the easier it will be for you to set your priorities straight and 'weigh-up' things in your favor. To reach that stage where your ideal self-persona matches who you are, you can employ different strategies such as:

- Making up a mind map
- Maintaining a journal with a picture or a timeline of your progress
- A vision board that inspires you to achieve more each day

The context of your persona and how far you want to stretch it lies in your hands. To feed and build your persona, you need to give your mind the positive input. This can include reading quality books, listening to podcasts, being in touch with current affairs, and opening up your mind to quality information sources and staying up-to-date with the latest breakthroughs.

You can also negatively invest in your persona by being around negative people, indulging in criminal activity, and just focusing on being the most disrespectful person you can be. The investment that you make in your personality is far more than what you acquire through formal educational degrees. When you consciously invest in yourself, you have a profound impact on your surroundings and the people who are directly or indirectly connected to you.

You either choose to equip your mind with the necessary knowledge, skills, and resources that will bring you in the limelight, or you are the kind of personality that lies on the other side of the spectrum, where you would prefer to take the back seat and lay low than being noticed. This is when you have to *"weigh it up."* That's when you shift your attention from growing and building your persona to fueling your ideas to achieve something so great that it becomes central to your existence.

You could channel your energies in expanding your career. The same way a person's persona can grow from something very inconsequential (as minute as an ant) to something that baffles the human mind. I've noticed people's brain and intellect have the capacity to expand beyond measure to the point we surprise ourselves at the end of the day.

For some, the definition of success is to reach the status where they are featured on a billboard or considered for a caste on TV. For others, it is just about being successful in their surrounding space, and between their inner circles is enough. Either way, it's all perceptive on how much someone wants to invest, build, and grow their personas.

Fuel Your Ideas

So if an idea or career can grow in the same way, you grow your persona. You have to let the idea grow and continue to feed it until it realizes its true potential. It may take an idea a lifetime to substantiate into something meaningful and reach the status that you expect it to reach.

It's very well possible that you will not be able to see the scope of how big your idea is and the capacity that it contains till you look at it from a broader view.

You have to expand your horizons and have the ability to look through the roadblocks and view it from a third-person perspective. You could be close to your destination but yet on the verge of giving up. How will you know that you are almost there if you do not keep refreshing your perspective and see things from a different angle?

When you are working in the middle of your ideas, sometimes you cannot see what everyone else sees because you're too close. You may have to step away from your work and take a look at what you're doing. It's essential to get a realistic view of what you're doing.

Progressive thinkers try to do things differently. They try to bring in the laser-focus through fresh eyes and brainstorm combinations that are not mainstream. They step back to gain perspective, believe in experimentation, and carry the ability to sail through potentially intimidating environments to be able to reach the pinnacle of their career or bring their ideas to life. For example, if you're painting a wall canvas, and the wall is 20 feet wide by 20 feet tall, you can't possibly see the scale of your work accurately until you step far enough back away from it to get the view of the entire wall.

So, as you paint, you will need to make trips back and forth from the project to continue your critique and accuracy. When the final picture is ready, you wouldn't be witnessing something that you were not prepared for. Your business, persona, ideas or vision will all require this same way of working for you to continue to grow. You don't want to work on this wall art for years and never step back to look at it, and all of a sudden one day when you finally step back to have a bird's eye view of the final picture, it is not what you were envisioning in your mind. Suddenly, none of it makes sense, and the outcome in front of you is far from what you had imagined. You cannot say that I can't see what I am doing, none of this makes sense, and I'm tired, and just walk away and quit the canvas you are painting. You need to own up to your work and think of ways to fix this as now it's just an eyesore for others. Take ownership of whatever you're doing. However, due to a lack of vision, if you abandon the project in the middle, someone else has to come up and assume responsibility to cover up for it. Someone else has to reattempt to paint the wall portrait because you quit mid-project. All because your vision wasn't big enough. You couldn't see the scope of your work. You couldn't get inspired anymore because you couldn't see what you were doing.

Surround Yourself with Positive, Constructive People

This is where you allow the right people to step in!

Positive, proactive people who lift you in smoky times!

People who want the best for you and are your well-being!

People who make you feel like you're Appreciated and Valued!

The people you have around you can assume many different roles. They can help you, lift you, propel you, watch over you, supervise you or they can try to discourage you, ignore you, entertain you, and distract you. Each role that the people around you assume can be both detrimental and uplifting for you in the long run. Keep in mind, the people in your life are very crucial in contributing to your overall persona and image.

Make sure you're okay with the role of others in your life. One of the most central aspects of building anything worth having includes networking with the right kind of people who project a sense of positivity. Never underestimate how important having the right energy around you can be. People who treat you with kindness and respect do a great favor in strengthening your confidence and vision for your ideas. They would never demean you or look down upon you in the worst of their moods and exercise their highest level of maturity when dealing with the ugly phases of your life.

The amount of self-belief that you build within yourself is highly dependent on the forces around you in the form of people you choose and the experiences that you go through. In this fast-paced world, full of cut-throat competition, the least you can do is support a circle that is free of fear, negativity, and stress. You need people who are supportive of your ideas and help you idealize your dreams. The company you keep is a true reflection of who you are. It is definitely not worth investing in people who only drain you of your energies as they sabotage your perspective and low-key disrespect you.

Your vibes attract your tribe…

As Jim Rohn says: *"You're the average of the five people you spend most of your time with."* The more positivity you surround yourself with, you will develop a more optimistic approach to life. Whether we talk about the staff that you hire at your workplace – be it on a management level or clerical level, they influence the overall culture of the organization. Being a business owner for many years now, I've noticed that it is very important to filter out the people who truly represent your organization's corporate values and ethos. It is essential to recognize and separate out who can justifiably present themselves and your business in the light that you want to be portrayed.

Sometimes you may hire an employee who is technically sound and is also proficient at his work, but his negativity just seems to build an environment of mistrust and pessimism, which is detrimental for the organization's overall growth and prosperity. That is when you have to make the hard decision of letting some people go who, although may be very good at their work, their ideas, thoughts, and behaviors are not in line with what you intend to propagate through the company.

That is when you have to decide the cut-off that will determine whether you are going to retain that employee or fire them. Sometimes you have to weigh up the pros and cons and judge based on professionalism. Even though the decision that you take at the moment may feel like one taken in a hurry or impact the bottom-line due to a loss of technical expertise but it will undoubtedly help block out the negativity that that person was bringing to the table.

Indeed, when a person has been at the establishment for so long, and people are so attached to them, it never is a good feeling to imagine how things will be once they are no longer there. However, the shocking part is it always works out so much better in the end because there is nothing more valuable than mental peace. Sometimes it is not only about the financial gain or loss at the end of the day as some people are more of a liability than an asset. The negativity, skepticism, and uncertainty that certain people bring with themselves are not worth risking at all for anything. When the environment becomes free of these toxic people once and for all, you realize that you are much better off without them. The same applies to the people in your circle.

"People who add value to others do so intentionally. I say that because to add value, leaders must give themselves and that rarely occurs by accident."

-John C Maxwell

When you are stepping into a new phase in your life, embarking on a new life journey or beginning your career – you need to thoroughly weigh out the negative, toxic people lest they suck out the energy from within you. Being in control of the present moment and your future, you must prioritize what truly matters and do not get stuck in between people who do not value you as a person. You need to identify the energies that uplift you and the ones that are not good for your productivity.

It's better to walk alone than to surround yourself with people who are full of negativity and are continuously thawing away at your determination to reach your highest level of success. The mission to finding and focusing on relationships who would celebrate their wins with you is real! Not only that, but they also help you achieve greatness in your own life and not feel any less. Sometimes, it's not necessary that your vibe matches the other persons but can always fine-tune your approach and weigh out things that are not in sync with what you want in life. Sometimes you can invest your energies in people and bring them under leadership to get their energies together. Getting the hang of a positive or a negative feeling is in your hands, and you need to decide which direction to steer in.

This is a great opportunity to establish what I call a war buddy. A war buddy is someone who is in the trenches with you. They were with you on your journey 100% of the way, and they have your best interest as you have theirs. You have each other's back no matter what, helping you battle through ups and downs and getting to your true potential. A help me help you person. Having multiple close team-mates who knows how to capitalize on your strengths and make-up for your weaknesses is a blessing in disguise.

Its human nature to take your company for granted. We all need people, whether it is your close family circle, friends, teachers, or mentors who challenge you to push yourself to the maximum that you can so that you can give your best. The importance of surrounding yourself with the right influence can help raise the bar higher for yourself and set loftier expectations of yourself, surprising yourself in new and game-changing ways. Weigh it up and get rid of all the negativities!

Chapter 4
Balance Your Scale

"Pay attention to whom your energy increases and decreases around. That's the universe giving you a hint of who you should embrace and who you should keep away from."

-Diddy

In Chapter 2, I made special emphasis on how it is so important to focus on establishing who you are first. People gravitate to you based on your energy, also known as the 'persona.' To reiterate this theory, you need to keep reevaluating who you are at the core and internalizing the values that define you.

If you intend to live a holistic life, you need to be able to look at the bigger picture and live life to the fullest. Constantly weighing the pros and cons of your actions and measuring everything you say and do on a calibrated scale as per your ideas and personality is vital to ensure that you are well-aware of the direction you are headed in. In the meanwhile, you also need to be appreciative of your efforts, journey, and how far you have come. What we say, do, take in, preach, and practice are all reflections of your inner voice and personality. Every so often, we all need to rebalance our lives. We need to stop and evaluate what direction we are going versus how much time it has taken us to get there. I call this rebalancing the scale. Bring every aspect to an equal viewpoint. Meaning, do the math and evaluate all areas of your life.

Good and bad, pleasant and unpleasant, uplifting or demotivating, and who are associated with your daily routine. Often holistically analyzing what life means being in a spiritual space that helps you fine-tune your body, mind, and soul to feel synchronized with the over-arching purpose and meaning of life.

However, there is a definition beyond that, which encompasses having a deeper understanding of how your actions do not only affect your life but also how the effects spread out to those around you and are felt by the environment as well. Establish a reason to connect with people on a higher level than you are used to. Step out of your comfort zone and take up activities that will help you broaden your perspective and meet like-minded holistic people. The new and positive energy in your life can push you to break boundaries that you never thought you were capable of overcoming. You can start by doing research on things you're interested in and just show up to events surrounding that subject.

Practically anything that interests and evokes a level of new territory seems to have subsided due to you being too comfortable. Join a course to enhance your skills or look up for light-hearted standup comedy shows or online Facebook groups that have like-minded people forming a community. Learn from people and connect with people who you feel are sailing in the same boat and can 'relate' to your journey.

These people have an inexplicable way of making you feel like you're a part of a larger ecosystem and how it is perfectly normal to feel a certain way. This rebalancing of the scale will help you bring things into perspective and not dwell upon things and people that do not have significance in your life. It can also make you realize that there is more to life than just a repetitive and robotic 9 to 5 life, so you need to have the vision to explore unchartered waters and gain an insight on how you can do things differently to be the best version of yourself. This is also a great opportunity to get in a cramped space again, keeping in view that discomfort is a sign of growth. Being uncomfortable keeps you focused and sharp. Contrary to that, comfort is unsafe as it makes you complacent and, to some extent, makes you self-absorbent and discontent. Since you have never ventured out of your comfort zone, you do not know how it feels to live a life full of risk and excitement—the power of the adrenaline rush that can make you accomplish things beyond your imagination.

"Nobody ever died of discomfort, yet living in the name of comfort has killed more ideas, more opportunities, more actions, and more growth than everything else combined. Comfort kills!"

-T.Harv Eker

Considering how much knowledge you carry in your mind, or how many years of experience you have under your belt, growth is something that everybody hopes for – the natural ability to improve consistently and put your best foot forward. Your comfort zone is that private space that limits your ability to explore yourself, where your behaviors are predictable, and fit a set pattern or routine, making you a risk-free person overall. Growth, on the other hand, requires you to get uncomfortable. As they say, there is no gain without pain – which follows that if you limit yourself to a feeling of familiarity and comfort – you're never going to take that leap of faith and take yourself by surprise. You will always fail to explore the greatness you have. You are neglecting one of the most potent and eye-opening experiences that life has to offer. If the people around you are not challenging you, then you may have to challenge the narrative and reboot the motivation of the relationship or find new friends and associates.

This is because you need to have that dose of creativity around that will propel you to discover the hidden potential to 'rebalance the scale.' The whole purpose of this exercise is to identify the gaps and loopholes that are deterring you from reaching your true potential and devising a strategy to mitigate it.

You don't necessarily want to just walk away from established relationships you have with your friends. It literally will depend on how you feel about what's going on. Still, sometimes people aren't interested in moving to the next level of success and achievements because they have seen and witnessed some minor levels of success. They may be happy where they are. Wanting more can be overwhelming for some, and they try to avoid the confrontation of discomfort. However, again growth begins at the end of your comfort zone!Comfort certainly does kill your productivity along with your creativity. You are so used to being in that safe space that your mind and body look for the default routines. We tend to show an inclination towards where we feel the safest. In truth, discomfort is what sets us on the path of breakthrough ideas, discipline, and a more refined way of approaching things.

If you don't make a conscious effort to reconsider your dynamics with yourself and the people around you, you end up picking the path that seems most comfortable. In the process of residing in your comfort zone, you tend to lose out on enlightening moments that can turn good into great. Sometimes, This includes mindlessly surfing through social media when you could spend the same time meeting your deadline or brainstorming new goals. It also infiltrates into your routine, reactions, and behavior with people, where you decide whether to take the back seat or address issues head-on. You have to reevaluate everything from your workspace to your private space to every other area or preoccupation that takes up time in your day. This is possibly the moment you take more chances in life. Take more risks than you ever have before. Take yourself more seriously than you ever did before. Project your vision more aggressively to new people. Make a decision on whether or not they want to support you, and when I say make a decision, I mean it literally!

In this highly connected world, it is very easy to define your own comfort zone and just stay there to avoid going through the intimidation and uneasiness of seeking out meaningful, deeper relationships with people who would fit your definition of 'like-minded individuals.' It's completely normal to make do with the people and friends circle that you have ultimately become a part of overtime. People seldom think of branching out and forming associations that would enrich them intellectually or spiritually.

However, once you explore this side of your personality, you will realize that there is nothing more uplifting and empowering than taking up the challenge of reading someone's mind and finding mutual interests and then reaching an agreement on how to do things. Do not underestimate the power of spending time with like-minded individuals! I repeat, surrounding yourself with like-minded, productive people is the key to developing a positive mindset!

You need to have it clear in your mind.

Does your crew support you? Are they supportive of your vision and life goals? Do they uplift you when you get second thoughts about what you are capable of achieving? Do they have those positive vibes that make you feel like defying all the boundaries and believe in the power of your dreams? Do they add value to your life? If not - they need to keep it moving.

The ultimatum can be harsh, but it's necessary. You must spend time with likeminded individuals to get your goals accomplished. Remember, you've just spent a huge portion of your time establishing and building your credibility to the people that are around you. So if they do not notice your efforts at this point, they most likely never will. Connecting with people whose brain wave matches yours is conducive to ground-breaking ideas. A safe zone where you can be yourself and share ideas almost instantly; it is like an incubator for your ideas. It gives you the confidence to speak your mind without the fear of being judged. That is something that not only de-stresses you but also makes you believe in the power of connection. Our minds are able to form many complex relationships at one time, and the more uplifting they are, the more productive you are. Many people prefer to be an observer or a critical spectator instead. And there is absolutely nothing wrong with that either. Of course, unless you are spending the majority of your time sharing information with them, that is unnecessary and not important to them.

Meanwhile, you could focus on all the others in your life that do see and respect your vision and assist you in any way they can. These are your original war buddies that have come so far with you and have not wavered in their intentions. These are the people who will give you an honest opinion about whether you are thinking in the right direction, support you in your bold steps towards accomplishing your tasks and make sure that you are not alone when life is doing too much. They stir conversations that are thought-provoking and mind-boggling and get you to collaborate on projects that create a win-win situation for both parties. Meeting up with such people often turns out to be pretty productive as they reinforce your ideas and propel you forward, standing behind you as a pillar for support. This is possible when you prove to them that you value them on an entirely different level, and you are now willing and ready to show that in more actions - actions that require your involvement. Meaning, if you are not taking any legal or financial action on your goals due to the uncertainty in the market, your war buddy will either support you or get you to find another alternative, but will never let you give up.

However, you're willing to risk everything with the right people because they have earned your trust. Do you trust them with your life savings? Maybe you can assist them by investing in their vision to get things going. It requires you to trust them enough to bet on their talent. This would be the time to make a move like that. That's why you have taken the time to establish this credibility and understanding with these people. I'm a firm believer that you cannot get anything done without the right people. It's always been that way in the world we live in. This is the best time in history to work with others because it's the 'futuristic age of social media platforms' designed to network with whomever. The convenient and empowering world of social media helps us understand the bigger picture and helps you align your metrics of success and goals accordingly People who are connected are more likely to climb the ladder of success in a shorter span of time.

When you are connected, you are more likely to learn from each other and help lift each other up. You don't have to partner with people who seem to be working hard, but in reality, don't make any real progress. You need to team up with people who work smart and hard at the same time.

The best physical network team wins. The better you work with your peers, the better performance you and your team can achieve. Everyone has to know and understand their positions and their specific role in the organization. Let the attorneys be attorneys; that's what they are good at, and let accountants be accountants.

If we assume our roles and discharge our duties efficiently, there will always be power and no confusion regarding what is to be done. A successful organization is one where you retain the core competencies and outsource the less critical or menial tasks that you do not have a command over. Investing your energy in work that you are not an expert in can lead to wastage of time and unproductive results. You should concentrate on what really matters and work in collaboration with people of all kinds to help give meaning to your efforts. Everyone will have a role to play in your life as they all have meaning and a purpose. We have to respect each other for who they are. As already established, you need to be aware of yourself inside and out and identify the intrinsic and extrinsic motivators that drive you. People gravitate to you based on your energy. The vibes that you exude will ultimately determine your crew and how you, as a team, get along.

A diverse team allows people to make up for each other's weaknesses and capitalize on each other's strengths. Then, with enough time going in the same direction, trust can be established. This will be a rinse-and-repeat action for the rest of your life, most likely. Ultimately it will keep you moving in the right direction for permanent results. With time, people find themselves in a different mental and spiritual space, and that needs to be addressed by reevaluating your relationship with that particular individual. If you stay back in time and do not give the other people the benefit of the doubt for evolving with time, it would get harder to rebalance the scale. You need to take into account all the factors that affect your relationship with your peers and weigh out any factors that can be a potential hindrance in your way.

When you rebalance your scale, these are the moments when you decide whether your glass is half full or half empty. It's nothing wrong with either if it's half and half. But you have a chance now, to be honest with yourself. Some people spend their entire life in a delusion and not seeing their actual situation for what it is. Accepting the reality of life is very important to keep yourself grounded and save yourself from unnecessary disappointment, regret, and uncertainty. Failing to realize the reality can have some drastic consequences for you. For this, you need to be able to:

- Accept who you are, just the way you are. Appreciate unconditionally and embrace all your imperfections. Self-acceptance can be a hard safe to open, but you need to learn to come to terms with what life throws your way and not try to push yourself in the opposite direction.

- Acknowledge your present situations and try to make the most of it. When you consciously internalize your situation, you learn to work wisely for a brighter future.

- Do not evade your problems or any controversial things in your life. Take your time to think it through, but make sure that you address the issues so that it does not grow bigger to be a more significant roadblock in the future. Practice radical honesty at all times. Lying to yourself won't get you anywhere.

- Identify your role in your personal space as well as the professional environment. Do not shun away from your responsibilities and own your outcomes. Do not let the fear of the unknown or uncertainty get in the way.

Don't mistake trying to keep a positive mindset with identifying real problems in the way. Figuratively speaking, when you get a brand new scale and take it out of the box, it should be zeroed out and perfectly balanced. After some time, the inside mechanisms may start to get a little off-centered. So proper maintenance will be needed to keep your scale well-balanced. Each of us is the center of our universe, and everyone else is revolving around us. So knowing where you are standing at all times is essential.

If you are considerate enough, you need to be able to evaluate the impact that you are casting on others and not be selfish by just thinking about your own mental space. Not being concerned about the people revolving around you can be from a place of extreme comfort. This analogy can be applied to our lives, where we need to stop in our tracks and reevaluate the various dynamics governing our life. If any of the major factors governing your life are going out of hand, you need to re-adjust your vision and set yourself up for success. You cannot keep ignoring the signs that life sends your way. That can be toxic for growth.

Remember, I said you want to be at a discomfort most of the time because that means you're continually growing. This is all about perception at this point. If you look at the cover of this book very carefully, you will notice in the detail that the scale has a compass on one side and a clock on the other. At a glance, it is perceived that the time reads 9:30. In reality, the hour hand is off by 30 minutes. The clock is not showing the right time and is creating an illusion. If you caught that, congratulations, you're on point. However, what matters here is how you perceive what you see. 9/30 is actually my birthday, which gives that clock on a Libra Scale an entirely different meaning to me. We all have a different eye when viewing things, which is why it is important to consider everyone's point of view when working as a team. On the Cover of this book are three items, and they are measuring devices; one measures weight, another measures time, and the final one measures direction. They're all equally important in whatever situation they may be needed for but operate differently from one another. In my opinion, similar to life, we all see things differently and operate differently, but everyone is equally important when trying to establish our position and point of view.

Making strong and substantial efforts to bond with like-minded individuals can help you in the long run and help you see things in a different light. A third opinion always gives your mind the ignition that it needs to propel you forward. If you want to make use of the unique qualities of every team member, you need to know how to balance the qualities of each one of them.

"The important thing is that your teammates have to know you're pulling for them, and you really want them to be successful."

-Kobe Bryant

Chapter 5
Document the Gains and Losses

When was the last time you used conscious introspection to evaluate your current standing? When did you last make a record of your accomplishments to put a value on what you've achieved? When did you last gauge your relationship with your profession?

More often than not, we are so engrossed in the daily tasks that we tend to lose track of our accomplishments and the lessons that we learn from our failure. However, you can regain that focus and get a perspective on life by journaling. Penning down how you feel about the present moment, the lessons that you bring along from the past, and how you can take a proactive approach towards the future can help you provide a safe space for your thoughts and actions. It also enables you to reflect on what you have accomplished so far and helps you appreciate your journey. How do you think we know what our ancestors went through and their way of life? If there were no way to document their lives and experience, we would never get an insight into how we have evolved differently from our ancestors.

The written word is hands down the most crucial aspect of educational history known to man. Without our ancestors documenting our past, we most likely wouldn't be as knowledgeable as we are. I couldn't imagine trying to learn information about everything without some references to the proper documents for dialogue and illustration.

Our ancestors have passed down to us many precious learnings that help us mold our lives around specific core beliefs and concepts that are central to our existence. If these values were not transferred down to us, we would be living a completely different life. Sometimes you just have to read about things to understand it, especially if you weren't physically there to see it. When you write something down, scientifically, it starts taking shape physically. The universe has a strange way of producing when action is applied. It will assist you if you start the process. The first form of physical growth begins in your mind. The second physical form that takes place is verbal. Whatever you keep thinking about, it repeats and keeps feeding your mind; that is what inevitably manifests itself in your personality. Writing down something helps you consciously acknowledge your state of mind, and you start working towards it more aggressively and categorically.

What you write gets etched to your existence forever, and the world gets to know about it. It's no longer a secret once it's documented. The energy it takes to write starts to produce the actions it requires for things to happen. That's why you write your goals down. I'm not exactly sure how the law of attraction works, but I think it's along the same lines as writing and documenting the things you're doing.

"When you write down a goal, no matter how big, or impossible it seems, you activate a series of forces in the universe that often make the impossible possible."

-Brain Tracy

Commit To Your Goals to Write

It's not rocket science to understand why writing down your goals can help you accomplish it more efficiently and with greater determination, because having it laid down in front of you can greatly speed up things. You will have a clear picture of what you want in your mind. Unless you have the final destination chalked out in your mind, how will you prepare and equip yourself to reach it efficiently? What is the path that you take if you do not have a set goal to follow and attain? For a fact, writing down where you want to go will help you identify the milestones along the way and tackle any roadblocks that may be a hindrance.

Goals, when written down, give your life meaning and shape. Oftentimes, you are bombarded with opportunities. To catch the relevant ones and let the less important ones go, you must have a list of all your goals in front of you. This way, you can ward off competition and filter out opportunities that are not absolute necessities. One of the best feelings in the world is to have the opportunity to check off the goals that you have achieved as it will help you look through your achievements and celebrate your progress. Written words will help you track your progress and provide concrete proof of how far you have come. You also get a chance to get hyped up and get yourself ready to work towards your next agenda. A famous example that is living proof of how documenting your goals can help you achieve them is one by Martin Luther King Jr. When he made his most memorable *"I Have A Dream"* speech in 1963, He projected the idea that his four children will not be judged by the color of their skin but by the content of their character, and his goal was printed down innumerable times by the press across the globe.

By documenting his vision, Mr. King made sure that his speech was felt by the masses and provoked a sense of responsibility upon the nation. We all are forever inspired to continue his vision and build upon it. Even though this is a macro-level example, we tend to apply this philosophy in real-life situations as well, where we need motivation or some kind of supervision to stay on top of our goals.

Writing down goals has a psychological effect on our mind, as we can pin them around the house, on the fridge, on a soft board or on our work-station, serving as a constant reminder of what needs to be done. With an exodus of information constantly bombarding our mind, highlighting the gains and losses we go through will help us adjust to accomplish milestones and put us in the right space of mind and stay on high alert to refocus when necessary.

Documenting Your Journey

If you have finally met with the opportunity that you have been seeking all your life or are about to kick start a lucrative venture, now is the time to take things in your own hands. Now is the time you start maintaining a journal that will have a timeline of your milestones and accomplishments over time. Every challenge that you encounter helps you stretch your limits and enhance your learning curve. Encountering a problem may also lead you to rummage through your mind and come up with ideas that will make you realize your true potential.

Whether you are an entrepreneur, a small-business owner, or a student geared towards accomplishing your deadline, having a journal with charts and diagrams will help guide you better and build your knowledge base. You can then leverage this repertoire of information and tools to assume the role of mentor and impart your valuable experience to others so that they may learn something new, too, from your journey. Often, we try to recall that one crazy idea that we thought could turn the trajectory of your life. But when you get bogged down by other trivial matters, the idea tends to get lost somewhere. That is when you realize that even though our creative mind was where the idea was born, it is not necessary for us to retain it and remember it for an extended period.

These enlightening insights and ideas need to be preserved so that you can practically implement them to prove your point. Taking your innovative and creative thought process for granted can make you miss out on a lot of key parameters that you can base your success on. Consciously acknowledge the thoughts and ideas that come to your mind and make a concerted effort to write them down for future reference.

Sometimes the time and situation might not be right to implement a certain idea. Later on, when you are in a different physical and mental space or when you have the resources, you are able to work on your ideas and give them some direction and meaning. Back in 2009, I came across some information that explained how important a journal was. At the time, I wasn't into writing anything down, but I went out and purchased an empty book. I paid over $30 for this blank book because I figured that a nice journal would make me want to fill it up faster with information and value-added learnings. I wanted to personalize this journal with whatever I could think at first so that I would have something to look back to. I started writing every day after work, and as the pages started to fill, It started to feel similar to going to the bank and putting money in my account. I wrote about each day, and what happened that day and what I went through.

During this time of writing, I think I went through a lot. Truthfully, though, it wasn't that, I've been through way worse. The point was that I actually had it documented. I was able to go back and read about all the details of those days that entire year. It was wild and highly reflective of valuable information. It's not that I went through more than I ever did before, it's just that when I was able to go back and read about it, it was very eye-opening to me. I was able to read about how I handled certain similar situations that I later needed advice on. It made me more mindful of my actions and how I needed to be more present in the moment to engage with people around me. It helped me avoid past mistakes and do things differently in the future. Our focus shifts from a more personal perspective to objective awareness of the situation; it's like viewing your life from a third-person perspective and gives the ability to make decisions from a brighter, unbiascd lens. Writing things down makes us more aware of everything that's going on and identify certain patterns in our behavior.

This helps us become more aware of how we react, whether proactively or reactively. Rather than giving in to the habit, having a mindful thought process can help you reconsider your response before reacting. You need to sharpen your self-reflection skills to get the keys to the doors.

I continued to write throughout the years about troubling and good times, but not like the year of 2009. Now I just write in the journal once and a while just to capture certain moments. At the least, I can pass that information down to my son, and it will be useful to him way after I'm gone. But the point is, it was so helpful to see that I've been through some extreme times, and I can always remind myself that if I made it through that, then I can make it through this. Your head is already filled with lots of thoughts about various thoughts that can be referred to as 'mental clutter.' Finding a safe space outside your mind where you can unload your thoughts and bring yourself to peace can do a great favor for your mental health. I assume it's similar to musicians writing lyrics and then making a song. Getting those ideas out and then making songs may end up being very productive for them.

Debunking myths and letting the troubling thoughts go can put your mind at peace and prevent it from going into the self-sabotaging mental loop that messes up with your thinking and undermines your productivity levels. Clarity of mind is something that can help you elevate your productivity levels and help you realize when it is due for evaluation. Your past thoughts lingering around for too long can lead to a vicious cycle of negativity.

The major effects of documenting cannot be underestimated when it comes to psychological health as well. This is mostly known as reframing your personal narrative. Having the internal capacity to reflect back on your core ingredients, thoughts, behavioral patterns, and experiences is like coming to terms with your own story. There is no point in being in denial and not accepting life's harsh realities. When you are ready to face your life story with unwavering determination and purpose, it makes it easier for you to come to terms with it. You can then edit, clarify, and change your narrative accordingly at any time. Literature is something that I'm starting to have a lot more respect for because the world is moving so much faster nowadays. You can only write so fast and read so fast. The modern era is one that demands information sharing to be able to keep up with the times and spread out to help shape a culture of honesty. It's one of my reasons and motivations for writing this book.

One benefit of documenting your journey is that you get a chance to establish your POV - your 'point of view' of the world. In business, I realized that the better I'm able to communicate my point of view, the better it would be for my associates to understand how I think. It's important for my peers and for me to know how I think. It can help by giving them the opportunity to know me on the levels beyond business. They can compare my persona to my written word and weigh it up. They can tell if I'm genuine with my words and actions. Does it all balance out? Knowing someone personally, on a deeper level, helps forge that connection and bond that can help you understand them in other walks of life. If a business person stays true to his ethos and values, knowing him on a surface-level versus knowing him holistically will reflect in the way they deal with each other. I don't want my character in question for anything in regards to my word. My word is literally all I've been able to stand behind for years. When there was no money, all I had was my word. When you have nothing but your word, you tend to take it seriously and expect others too as well. If you don't have that, you're pretty much in a jam out here. I know I can trust myself if no one else does. I document my journey. It's all true. If I ever need to remind myself about where I'm trying to go in life or where I came from, all I have to do is check my notes.

This is a very empowering feeling as you are at peace with yourself that what you are doing is not blurred by any irrationality. There are several ways to judge someone's worth, and one of them is to *"keep your word."* Words have the power to make or break someone's trust in you and hold immense power over us. It can convince us to trust our instinct and can also lead us apart from someone whom we held in high regard. Words are a reflection of your personality and personal value. You're only as good as your word. People take you at face value. It is up to you how you live up to people's expectations and set the bar high when it comes to dealing with people in personal and professional settings. Every business that I have ventured into, we had to get a business license approved from the state. That business license certifies businesses. Technically, without it, you have no business even if you think you do. I treat my writing the same way. I do not consider myself a great writer, and I don't write everything down. It's not practically possible as it requires considerable time, but I do try to write down ideas that I might forget.

There have been certain moments in my life where I have felt the dire need to reflect back, check on my notes, and tally it with the situation going on. On further investigation, I realized that sometimes using my notes as a point of reference has made me feel so thankful for documenting my journey, as it helped me realize who I am. Budging from my values was not an option at all because our values are what make us who we are. Another great form of documenting can be photos or videos. Capturing certain moments that may seem inconsequential can actually have a lot of significance in your life and may have a personal value attached to it. Photographs have this magical way of freezing moments and preserving a portion of our past accurately. Occasions such as parties and anniversaries, or a promotion celebration can stay in our memories. In my perspective, I consider this executive producing. By maintaining a repository of photos that leads back to a pivotal moment in time. It's almost like watching your own movie. It can trigger a thought or idea that you forgot about.

When it comes to documenting and preserving these moments, Social media platforms have come a long way and evolved in a very creative and innovative way by giving us a platform to showcase our story. Social media may seem biased at times, but the trend of posting pictures and videos have given us a creative space to experiment with our sense of taking pictures and committing it to public scrutiny. Social media believes in the truth, but we have mastered the art of manipulating data in our favor and indulging in showing ourselves in this race of proving who is better than the other. Sure, you should preserve those moments, but you should keep in mind that it is only for the purpose of keeping a log and not to consume yourself for the sake of social validation. It also helps establish a point of reference if necessary. Of course, I could not post pictures, but I've captured moments in my good mental space along with my bad mental space. Mainly for communication purposes and the creation of an image for myself. It is important to have a credible persona in which people see and build a perception now. It also helps you track your journey over a span of time and see how far you have come. For me, It's more for my own research on how society works and responds to actions these days.

They do say a picture speaks a thousand words. Have you ever looked at a picture and pondered how much time has fled, and things have changed since then? Pictures can give you the view that you can never see if you contain yourself to a nearsighted view and do not allow yourself to rise above the minuscule and inconsequential things that can blur your vision and deter you from seeing the bigger picture. Remember, it's good sometimes to step back and see yourself and your situation so that you can see things accurately. Well, pictures are a great way to get a view of your life from another angle and see what can be done differently. A third eye can help identify the gap holes that need to be filled and make suggestions for improvement. You can be critical of yourself just like everyone is; there's nothing wrong with positive criticism. You can record yourself on video or verbally document your thoughts to go back and see how far you've come. It's just important to have that point of reference at all times. It helps build your version of who you are in your mind and do justice to it. As we progress through life, we keep evolving and make value-added changes in ourselves so that we stay relevant with the times and not fall prey to insecurities.

It's all about learning from the past and making sure that you do not repeat the same mistakes again. Since you have everything documented, it is easier to look back and reflect on it and efficiently draw your conclusions. My accountant still possesses notes that she wrote in meetings that we had back in 2005. It's unbelievable and overwhelming to see how far we have come since we started off, and the timeline of our accomplishments gives us the boost to reach greater heights. Seeing those goals checked off, have been very helpful with mind and vision empowerment. Documentation is especially important when trying to establish structure. Anything significant and large enough eventually has to have structure. If it's not in place, it's a high chance; it will fall apart. We cannot manage our futures without complete sentences. We need to be in control of our lives and make sure that we take the necessary steps to steer our ship in the right direction. You are your own competition, and you only need to strive to be a better version of yourself when you are good at documenting.

Chapter 6
Tip The Scale

"I'm about seeing long-term, seeing a vision,
understanding nothing really worthwhile happens
overnight, and just sticking to your script long enough to
make something real happen."

- Nipsey Hussle

To Tip the Scale in the right direction, you need to have a vision that takes into account everybody's accomplishments, contributions, and point of view. Since the beginning of this concept, I have been stressing on the fact that tipping the scale is wholly and solely in your hands, and you need to make the necessary efforts in the right direction to develop that 'competitive mindset.'

Personally speaking, I am a person who believes in creating a win-win situation for my team members and me as well. If you want to make things work for you and develop that can-do, I-hate-to-lose-mind-set, you need to tune in your approach by keeping all environmental factors in mind. You need to take this seriously, as you cannot afford to fool around and not take your competition seriously. Some people do not like to come to the forefront and lead their team and make sure that they put up a tough fight to get everyone what they deserve. However, when it comes to me, I have quite a competitive mindset and believe that competitors push you to perform to your best. My visionary, forward-looking, and thinking has made me push the boundaries of time and think about things from an analytical perspective. Appreciating your competition will help you take them as healthy competition. It is but natural that nobody likes to lose, and I am certainly not fond of losing too.

However, to be a winner, it's a must to strategize accordingly as well. You need to be in the winning mode all the time. I think the way I am is because I have this passion and appreciation for the people around me. I always have this habit of going to any lengths to understand people and see how I can make things work for them. I consider myself to be a very good war buddy because I would give up anything to support my close circle of friends, family, and loved ones. Even when it comes to a professional setting, I won't leave any stone unturned in ensuring that everyone is heard and given an equal opportunity to put their best foot forward. If we meet with success in mind, it's not just one person who is responsible for leading the team but is a cumulative effort that puts you in the high-spirited mode and makes you achieve success as a team. Do you think it's crazy to take competition as a fuel to power your engine and will to achieve great heights? You need to be crazy, in my opinion, and passionate about winning to feel the adrenaline rush. Competition, in my opinion, is a contribution to the lifeblood of any business that wants to establish itself on firm grounds. I don't usually take out time to study competition and find out what they are doing.

I Embrace the uncertainties and let it ignite reactions so that I am adamant about overcoming them. Once you witness and feel success, it will propel you to stay on top of your mental game, and it is this unstoppable spirit and competitive mindset that will help you balance the scale and tip it in your favor. For me, success is not just individual progress but the attainment of team goals. If I buy a house, I want all my business partners to buy a house. If I get a Rolex, I want all my friends to have a Rolex. I wasn't always like this. I didn't establish this type of mindset until I got into business with others. I realized that I can't win without them and that they are my support system when it comes to reaching somewhere in life. I'm not afraid to admit that as I believe in giving due credit to anyone who deserves it. My genuine advice to everyone trying to foster an environment conducive to growth would be to make it a point to give proper feedback and establish a system of acknowledgment and reward.

Everyone deserves and seeks to get recognized for their efforts. Take out time to reward your teammates with proper awards that they have earned on the base of their merit. Do not take them for granted, because if you want them to build with you and the organization, you need to respect and value their efforts in bringing a substantial change. Celebrate you and the team's success in good spirit and ensure that your 'war buddies' feel valued. These are the people who are willing to break through and stand by your side no matter what. If you are ready to go to any extent for them, they will surely return that with their actions. When it comes to real-life implementation, it's not always about winning. In the practical scenario, to breathe life into an idea, you need to be prepared to face resistance and get thrown off by competitors. The struggle to reach your goal is real, and you must be prepared to deal with the challenges that come your way. Remember that we are talking about tipping the scale so that things turn out in our favor. This follows that you can never be in two places at the same time.

Either you are all up for a friendly competition, or you are on the opposing side. I can never put up this mask of being a hypocrite and giving fake smiles and pretending that you are a well-wisher. If you are not up for supporting someone in their dreams and life goals, you need to muster the courage to be true to what you feel.

I can admit that if I'm against you, I'm downright against you. It's an all-out war for me. I'm not interested in fake friendships and smiling faces that come along with people who want to compete but won't admit it. Call me old school, but I kind of live by the term; if you're not with me, then you must be against me. All of this is in good spirit, of course, considering I'm only talking about business on this topic for the most part. When it comes to business, you must get your priorities straight so that it does not impact your bottom-line. When having a professional relationship, it is important that you work on mutual understanding and make sure that the individual goals of the stakeholders are preserved. None of the partners thinks and acts in isolation. You cannot expect to steer in your direction without keeping in mind where the team wants to go.

Sure, you might have your unique approach and way of doing things, but that certainly does not mean that you can infringe on other people's ambition and crush it with your domination or inconsideration. You need to work collaboratively while forging unanimous opinions along the way. Even if there is any point of difference or conflict of opinion, it can always be negotiated and talked out rather than being toxic for each other's growth.

For example, my brother and business partner felt that he wasn't following his passion for becoming a DJ and had dedicated the majority of his time to his barber career. So, he insisted that he wanted to rethink his career after a six-to-seven-year commitment with our collaboration in the barber industry. After communicating this to me, we discussed the prospects of him pursuing his dream career alongside investing a decent time in the joint proposal that we were originally pursuing. We discussed the feasibility and weighed the pros and cons regarding how he would divide the time between his two involvements and try his best to strike a balance. We worked out a game plan together, and now he's able to do both businesses and fulfill his maximum potential. He didn't have to drop one to pursue his dream profession after all. That's the benefit of communicating and putting things on a scale so that you know how to weigh in and weigh out when things aren't in your favor. That could only happen because he involved me in his idea and plans. This displays a genuine war buddy.

If he had decided to stop working with me with no explanation at all or even start a new business in the same field, *"meaning the barber industry,"* things would have been entirely different. Our equation and brotherhood would be devastated because of a mere business disagreement.

It's not competition until you consider it competition

Any business venture that I have been a part of, I have always been interested in knowing who is my strongest opposition so that I can strategize my action plan accordingly. Researching upon them and finding what they are doing in their own space is very important for me to decide whether they are my allies or opponents. You can't blindly trust everyone in the corporate world as not everyone is rooting for you. You might be targeting the same niche and dealing in the same product or service, but I am more interested in the income and the overall impact the business has to offer to the world. I believe in making your business unique in its own way to stand out from the crowd.

I'm always deeply passionate about my ventures and consciously aware of who I am. Self-awareness is the first step to understanding what you want in life. This makes it easier for you to chalk out a game plan. I know if I'm prepared to go to war, and I know if I'm not. There's no in-between. I don't prefer spending my time in confusion or contemplation as I would never want to lose the opportunity in the moment and then regret it later.

That doesn't mean I'm throwing white flags, it just means I wouldn't write a check that I know my bank account can't cash. It's all about knowing the means and resources that you have at your disposal and not going over and above your defined ethical, mental, and say financial boundaries. What I'm mostly concerned and bothered about sometimes, is that I have seen this happen way too often. I see great talented people become competitors when there was such a great opportunity to achieve greatness together. They decide it would be a better move for them to be on the opposing team, which is perfectly fine. I'm just not sure what the motivation is at times. Sometimes I'm curious if it is a person, or is it simply that they can't envision the greatness that can be achieved with collaboration.

It's also very possible they don't want to share success with anyone in the same space, I don't have those anxieties because I understand the bigger picture now, respectfully. Mainly because of my work ethic, but, most importantly, because of my associates and business partners. You can't always find a like-minded individual who would like to join forces and take your business to another level. There will always be someone who will try to branch out to establish their entity and sabotage the joint efforts that you put. However, you need to make peace with it as the corporate world is full of uncertainty, and you can only do so much to control the factors that define your professional relationship. This is especially when both parties arc usually looking for the same results out of the situation. Sometimes it's tough to decipher and crack the code on where they see themselves in reaching a space that defines success. Either way, once they decide to compete, I'm all in. However, more than often, I have seen people out-rightly defy you in your journey and offer no sort of emotional, mental, or physical support. Even if they have no other preoccupations, they would rather sit idle but would make no efforts to assist you in your journey. That is when I wait to hear something about what they have accomplished in life, anything groundbreaking that would make me say that yes, they are doing something substantial with their life. If they ever cross my path, I would like to know what was so great that they were trying to achieve that they couldn't spare time to at least stand with me as a support and partner of strength.

Bringing Value to the Table

It's completely ok to have your own goals and purpose in life, be it in a personal or professional space. However, you need to keep in mind that you can't always be on the expecting end and have people invest in you all the time. Some people are in desperate need of real leadership – someone who can mentor them and give them the right platform to bring out their capabilities and contribute positively to society. Plain and simple. All sorts of people make the world, and you need to understand what kind of people need to be kept at arm's length so that they do not turn out to be toxic for your productivity.

They will come in to eat the full, well-prepared meal without making any considerable contributions during the cooking process. I hope this analogy makes you understand what I am trying to say. It might not connect entirely with what we have been talking about. Still, I considered it important to highlight the fact that you need to stop leeching off people's energies and taking undue advantage of their good nature and kindness.

It can be mistaken as weakness. If you can bring something to the table to achieve greatness with someone, then put your best foot forward and give it a real go. You never know what will come out of it as it's rare to find someone that cares about your well-being, so you should take them seriously if they want to work with you. But, I do realize this as well, and this is important to know. I can share this from a place of truth because I've been through it many times.

We are living in a world full of clutter, and we need to categorically identify what to invest in and what to let go of!

What are you doing to keep up with the times? What is it that sets you apart from the rest?

What is the value-addition that you bring in the lives of people around you?

Remember! In this cut-throat competition, the person who brings in value is the one who gets the benefit of the doubt in the situation and has the upper hand.

During an interview, we might assume the interviewer has the upper-hand, but little do we realize that if we bring value to the table, there is no reason for the interviewer to reject you or put you down. The interviewer is only looking for someone who can explain themselves and present their skills in the most efficient and presentable way. If you can convince the employer that you can bring real value to the table – there's no stopping what you are going for.

You only get a specific position or status in life when you earn or deserve it. You can't possibly dream or strive to be at a spot when you don't have the necessary knowledge or skills set to get it together. Many of the people that you expect to get involved in supporting your vision will often not be qualified actually to help you in any way. Maybe they do not have any background knowledge of the niche that you are operating in or have the least bit of interest in helping you at all. I've convinced myself, at times, into believing that people were more capable of doing things that I thought they could do, but it doesn't work that way.

For example, if I purchased a tow truck and needed a driver to drive it and pick up vehicles, the worst thing I can do is ask someone that hasn't even driven a vehicle before to drive the tow truck for me. Especially with no license to drive a commercial vehicle, I would be setting myself up for a lot of trouble and destruction. Wouldn't that be plain stupidity? Well, it's the same concept. If you are building a team, the people you build with have to be qualified.

You cannot ask people to do things that they are unequipped to do. You can't change a person's life unless they want to change. Change comes from within, and you can never force it on someone to be an agent of change. We have to keep our expectations in check and know where and how much to attach your expectations. It would only be equivalent to deliberately setting yourself up for disappointment if you expect from people, despite knowing that they are not capable of fulfilling them. I've expected things from people that I should never have expected. I've seen a lot of people make long term decisions based on their opinions and emotions while never realizing the real impact of their choices. I believe there are always two sides to the coin, and the coin can only rest on one side. Either it's true or false or right or wrong. When you start concentrating your efforts towards seeking the truth and filtering the people who have the sound technical expertise and the proper skills to make things work, that is when you are capable of setting the narrative.

You can't just boast of your capabilities and expect others to believe it unless you've established that credibly. I live by these same terms and make sure that if I am making a claim, I am capable of proving my mettle as well. I do not expect anyone to believe me unless I've earned that credibility on the base of my efforts and behavioral patterns. I prefer to prove to a non-believer. That's integrity. It's my North Star. I strive to prove my points and make every possible effort to achieve my set target so that people do not have any points that go against my narrative. Some people literally think that

I'm crazy, just because I've had big dreams that may seem impossible to them, but believing in the power of dreams is what drives and motivates me. When I find myself drifting into unrealistic territory with my words, I try my best to get back to reality and figure out a way to make things that seem impossible, possible. If I can see something that no one else can see, my whole mission in life is to help those people develop a perspective. In my opinion, your behavior and actions can very well compel and convince people to look at the bigger picture through your lens.

I also look forward to listening to other people's ideas and get enlightened. Remember, if you want to be heard, noticed, and acknowledged, you've got to be a good listener and take an equal interest in other people's ideas and give your valuable feedback to expect them to engage with you. That's ultimately been one of my most effective actions in getting my goals accomplished.

I try my best to bring value to the table. If I realize that I may be of no value to a situation, I'm most likely going to remove myself from the situation. It's either all in or all out. I believe in tipping the scale in the direction that best uplifts my motto and agenda in life, and that is a source of guidance and support for those who need it. My views and ideas come from how I've educated myself over the years. I've always had a relentless passion and an undying spirit to make the best use of the resources that I have and not go overboard with my expectations. I also look to see what value people bring into my life, who I let in, and who I block. We all have to be aware of our innate talents and how we can capitalize on them to propel ourselves towards unprecedented heights. This is where collaboration comes into the picture. When you are consciously aware of where your strength lies, you can easily work on them and present yourself in the best possible light.

However, in areas that you feel there is a lack, and you would need someone to cover it up for you, you collaborate with people to form a complete whole that makes things doable and accomplishable. I've worked with diverse personalities, and I am sure they would have established different opinions of me based on my working patterns, but I know one thing for sure and that is, I take my time to open up to others. It's like before venturing out into unchartered waters; I make sure to gauge the depth of the waters before I go on to forge some kind of bond with them. It's all about work ethic first. I have to see their work ethic and how strongly they believe in diligence and hard work being an essential ingredient for a moral benefit. If they rate higher on the work ethic scale, it is clearly depicted that they have an innate ability to strengthen their individual capabilities and will definitely bring value to the table. Meaning, I'm never in a rush to establish expectations from people because I'm trying to understand their character first. If I notice this person could possibly be toxic or an obstacle to what I'm doing, I keep conversation and information light and distant. I'm constantly doing an inventory for people who are closest to me so that I do not let our awareness down of people who might only harm our interests in the long run and wouldn't really be supportive of our goals and long-term agenda.

Chapter 7
Give Back

Sharing is undoubtedly a critical human trait that helps you evolve as a human being. The best way to go about sharing, regurgitating, and ingraining knowledge into your value system is to share it with the world. Sharing helps reinforce concepts and reproduce them in a comprehensive and palatable manner. When you believe in the power of sharing, you make every possible effort to find platforms to spread the word.

Well-documented experiences provide knowledge and clarity to people from all walks of life because what real-life situations and experiences can teach you, nobody else can. Without others putting their theories and experiences together for us to observe, we can find ourselves going through unnecessary triumphs.

When you take up the responsibility of sharing your knowledge with others, you are often faced with challenging situations that make you question your internal values and re-evaluate what you have learned. This also helps refine and filter your knowledge and enables you to learn even more.

When people question you, it forces you to rummage through your brain to explain your point, which makes sharing a worthwhile experience. When you open up to people, you make others comfortable to open up as well and share with you too. This fosters an environment characterized by collaboration, openness, information-sharing, and teamwork. Nothing parallels the advantage that sharing breeds in a personal and professional scenario the same.

People sharing all kinds of experiences, good or bad, pleasant or unpleasant, uplifting, or saddening – each experience can help us draw life lessons. People believe in perpetuating values that bring value to the table and form connectivity of thoughts, leading to something concrete. Content in story form is the most common way to share information as it successfully evokes the interest of the reader. It intrigues the mind and instills in them a sense of curiosity, leading them to dig deeper and enrich their knowledge base. The more the information is shared, the more people learn from each other and benefit each other as a community.

When other people acquire knowledge from you, they not only refine it but even validate it and expand upon it, where necessary. This authenticates the knowledge that you originally own and also helps fill in the loopholes and re-evaluate your approach. The quality of what you share also improves over time as people give in their constructive feedback. The reason why I go out of my way to help people or disseminate the knowledge I have in different ways is that sharing my knowledge gives me a feeling of inner satisfaction and contentment.

I attribute my success to the opportunities and experiences that I got along the way. Had it not been for the interactive sessions with my friends, peers, and colleagues, I wouldn't be able to get to the realness of my reality. The people who touched my life helped my gratification to discover myself, and I want to help others to reach a stage of self-awareness where they can freely mingle and communicate with the people around them.

Giving Back Is Beneficial

What is the first thought that comes to your mind when you hear any good news regarding your life? Don't you have the urge to share it? Doesn't that make the victory even more worthwhile? The same happens when you go through a trauma. Your instant reaction is to have a go-to person to vent out your emotional frustrations and get it out of your system. Such is the power of sharing. It strengthens you in inexplicable and unimaginable ways, equipping you with the will power and integrity to face your fears and problems head-on. At the same time, it also helps you understand the true meaning of accomplishment and happiness. If we did not have the option of sharing our emotions, experiences, and life learnings, we would be stuck in our bodies and mental space, only seeing things from a trapped view.

Giving back doesn't necessarily require you to be a great philanthropist or get involved in highly charitable activities. It can be your time, mental or spiritual capabilities that you feel can benefit the people and world around you. From something as small as picking up garbage off the sidewalk to contributing economically and financially to society – giving back can take many forms. Sharing has a unique way of making you feel empowered. It has a certain magic that comes with it. When you take the initiative to share a specific ground-breaking idea, thought, or piece of information with say ten people, you're reiterating that fact times ten. Consciously feeding your brain this information several times in a row embeds it deeper into your subconscious mind and equips you better for the future. When you adopt the habit of sharing your thoughts with people around you, you start to feel a change. Imagine introducing the people around you to untapped opportunities that they never knew existed. If we kept our knowledge strictly to ourselves, we would never be able to enlighten those around us and be stuck in the never-ending rut of the quest for knowledge. The more we learn and share our experiences, the greater part we play in serving the community and giving back to it intellectually.

Eventually, you have to dispel the myths that have been blinding your approach and adopt a proactive attitude that helps you discover yourself by opening to others. Self-learning is a never-ending process, and you will always feel like there is a deficit that can be filled by acquiring a new set of knowledge and skills. You need to be able to put it out there, what you believe and feel at the core of who you are.

Knowledge Increases with Sharing

I applaud anyone who takes out the time to give back by illustrating their thoughts and ideas, no matter the repercussions or ridicule that may come with it. It's tough but never worries what other people will think about you; in fact, be confident in your approach and make it a point to be the kind of person who is generous enough to spread knowledge. A person's philosophy is uniquely established by experiencing different situations. I encourage everyone to give back, in any form that suits them, from financial and economic contributions to public community service to their community. Giving back will always be a great gesture to those that seek such resources.

Having the habit of sharing instills the need for constant, in-depth research while accommodating a lot of viewpoints. This, in turn, is organized into one solid source of ideas that can add up for your knowledge as well. Always be open to ideas and believe in the power of knowledge-sharing. You can redefine the boundaries of innovation and collaboration in all walks of life. Case studies are sometimes established for this purpose as it helps future teams learn from their previous experiments and errors.

Knowledge can get redundant and obsolete, and it is necessary to keep refreshing your database of information. To stay up-to-date and relevant to the times, you need to establish this cycle of circulating knowledge so that any upcoming breakthroughs and advancements are noted and acknowledged. This does not only help preserve culture but also helps enrich it overtime. Knowledge-sharing should be encouraged at both individual and organizational levels.

The importance of innovation and creativity, linked together, cannot be overlooked in the highly-paced environment that we work in. Sharing of knowledge helps open minds to new levels and allows people to participate in healthy dialogue. This also helps cement teams together as they feel that their ideas are being acknowledged and valued. When teams are on the same page, they feel connected to a greater purpose. The best way to motivate the team is to establish clear lines of communication and ensure maximum information-sharing.

Give Back to Go Forward

Widening our circles by investing in other people is important to ensure that we are taking care of ourselves in the Realest way. It has been established that as you extend a helping hand to someone, in whatever form you can, you start seeing the world from a view that changes a lot of things for you. If you were to pay close attention, you would realize that we have been ingrained with the value and ethic of "*pay it forward*" since the beginning. Whether you are an entrepreneur or an employee, you tend to experience different things at all levels of life. If we share our setbacks and failures with the youth or the people yet to embark on this journey, we can save them from a lot of hassle and enable them to learn from our mistakes.

You should have enough consideration to let them learn through your experiences rather than exposing them to the uncertainties without prior training. We indeed learn the most significant lessons by stumbling upon roadblocks, but if certain incorrect decisions can be prevented, it should be done at all costs. It's like allowing the next generation to get learning lessons from the "*dummy tax*" that I have already paid. This way, we can help the new generations to stay away from mistakes that we made during the struggling phase. This is not only a professional gesture but also instills high work ethics and morals.

Time versus Direction

The concept of this book is my philosophy on Time vs. Direction. With the allotted amount of time that we all have available to us, moving in the right direction is important. We can let time slip by and then regret later that we did not plan out our lives at the right time. Time can be compared to grains of sand held in your hand. If you plan and execute your life goals on time, the chances are that you wouldn't have to panic at the last moment to hold it and not let it slip by too fast.

The minute you realize that too much time has passed by and you need to take control of your life, the tighter you will try to hold on to it, the faster it will slip through your fingers. You need to be very particular with how you treat time because if you do not respect it, time will not respect you either. Without time management, nothing makes sense, and it can control you. Time is undoubtedly the greatest equalizer in the journey of life. Nobody has more hours in a day than you do; it's just the approach that you take to ensure that the clock is in your favor. How you do that is entirely up to you to make things go smoothly. When you spend time moving in the wrong direction, it can be considered time wasted. By constantly paying attention to your results, this can be beneficial to gaining access to the correct direction. You might be very particular about your time and trying to utilize it to the best of your abilities, but until you ensure that you are moving in the right direction, we can never make 'real progress.'

What do I mean by 'real progress?'

In my opinion, real progress is when you are getting your return on investment (your investment being time) in a way that maximizes value in your life and enhances your productivity levels. When you consistently channel your time and energy in the right direction, that is when your efforts will produce results. You need to 'create a plan' and break down your project into manageable parts so that your time is worth investing into whatever that is. You need to learn to delegate, outsource, and automate specific agendas, so that you can ensure that you are moving in the right direction. Sometimes it is necessary to tip your scale and focus more on your time. Other times it will be necessary to tip the scale to focus more on the direction you are going. I am sure by now, you have understood the concept of tipping the scale in your favor and can successfully apply it to your life as you proceed through the book.

The main focus is to find the perfect recipe to combine time and direction and bring about permanent changes in your life. With the temporary nature of things overwhelming us from all directions, you must aim for something permanent. There is no single recipe for success that I know of, and it is entirely subjective, but what we need to understand is that things cannot always pan out the way we envision them to be.

That is what the entire concept of tipping the scale sums up; we have to act according to our situation. To weigh obstacles accurately, we need to categorically identify what we need to change and what is more desperately needed in our lives; time management or setting the right direction to follow. Besides, we need to establish a positive point of view by having a support network both personally and professionally comprising of people who are supportive of our agendas in life. It's also important to come to terms with the fact that it requires you to do some trial and error and learn from your mistakes. It is crucial to make the best use of time. Give yourself time to understand the balance that best suits your nature and situation. Set goals, document progress, and then make the necessary changes. Remember that time, once lost, cannot be regained, and making sure that you do not lose sight of the goal line will keep you moving forward in the right direction. I Genuinely believe these scriptures will help us all Make Moves for Permanent Results!

TIP THE SCALE

MERVIS J MILLER II

www.ingramcontent.com/pod-product-compliance
Lightning Source LLC
Chambersburg PA
CBHW021148090426
42740CB00008B/994